My Magical Garden

We have created this book not only to help children express themselves in a safe and loving way but also to help adults understand the child's emotions and how best to help them. It will help to strengthen the bonds of love and create a greater understanding of your child's needs as well as opening the doors of communication.

My Magical Garden allows children to work through any problems that may be occurring at home, school or other situations in their lives.

It will not only empower them but it will also help them to release any negative emotions that they may have been holding onto.

As your child goes through the pages of this book they will be making many choices. Each choice they make will have a meaning and is a reflection of what is going on in their mind.

The meanings can be interpreted by using the appendix at the back of the book and it will give you a better understanding of how your child is feeling, thereby enabling you to help them.

When your child has made their choices you will notice that two or three of the choices carry the same theme i.e more independence, more love, more quiet time etc. This becomes your main area of focus when helping them, although it is still important to take into account their other choices.

As your child is changing all of the time, we recommend they make their choices weekly or fortnightly so that you can see how things are going and if there have been any changes.

Love & Light

Terri & Jacqui
www.holistichealing4children.com
www.angelslovechildren.com

Introduction

Imagine you can make your own garden
One that you keep in your head
Somewhere to go whenever you want
Even when you're lying in bed.

You decide what happens in your garden
And you choose who you want to invite
You can dance with the beautiful fairy
Or even have fun with the Knight.

It is somewhere to go when you're happy
And somewhere to go when you're sad
You will always be safe in your garden
There is no room for anything bad.

So now you can start your adventure
With the pages that follow in this book
Just trust your feelings and choose what you want
Now you're ready, you can take a look.

Lights

Choose the colour you like the most
The one that feels the best
You'll find that there's just one
That stands out from all the rest.

Now imagine the colour around you
And then allow it to flow
Right from the very top of your head
Down to the tip of your toe.

Feel it pouring all over you
Washing your worries away
Now you're feeling nice and relaxed
And everything's feeling okay.

White Yellow Orange Gold Green Blue Indigo Purple Ruby Red Pink

Flowers

The flowers are all very beautiful
So it is very hard to decide
Which ones to put in your garden
And which ones to put to the side.

Will you want the Rose or the Daffodil
Or will you want the lovely sun flower?
Take your time and have a look
You are the one with the power!

Once you have chosen your flowers
Think about where they will go
Somewhere that needs lots of colour
A place where they can all grow.

Friends and Family

You can have anyone you want in your garden
A friend or maybe your mother
You can even have a talk with your teacher
Or make up a game with your brother.

You can invite them to play in your garden
Or you can talk about a problem or two
Whatever the reason for them being there
It's completely up to you!

So remember that this is your garden
And only the people you invite
Can come along and be with you
This is the garden's delight!

APPENDIX

Each item that your child chooses for their garden will have a specific meaning. Please see below the different meanings for each page in the book.

RAYS OF COLOURED LIGHTS

White — White represents purification, clarity and truth. Your child may need some time out and nourishing fresh produce. The body and mind needs to be cleansed through meditation, yoga, nature, breathing techniques & salt bath.

Blue — Blue represents calming, communication and balance. Your child will benefit from some down time. More quiet time is needed. They may also need to be given the opportunity to express themselves through art, music and nature.

Purple — Purple represents dreams, growth, and communication. Allow your child to be who they need to be. They need freedom to grow.

Indigo — The colour indigo represents your intuition and a general awareness of your surroundings. Your child would benefit from guided visualisations, breathing techniques or yoga.

Green — The colour Green represents love and nurturing. Your child needs to regularly be in nature, and have a nourishing fresh diet to bring about balance and harmony.

Pink — Your child needs to feel your love and affection at this time. Your child is feeling vulnerable at present and therefore needs to feel safe. Spend more quality time with your child.

Orange — You need to nurture your child's creativity and embrace your child's originality. Your child is warm, optimistic, friendly and good-natured. They need freedom to grow. Bring more creativity into your child's life.

Ruby Red — By choosing the colour Red your child may be tired, ungrounded or angry. If it is tiredness allow your child to rest. If its anger then your child needs help either through humor, re-direction or time out. If they are ungrounded they need to play in nature.

Yellow — Your child needs more joy, humor and lightness in their life. They need more choices, meditation and less electronic devices. Be spontaneous with your child. Have a day off from your normal routine.

Gold — Your child has lots of hidden talents and confidence. They would benefit by being in a peaceful and quiet environment from time to time to be able to tap into that inner wisdom and knowledge.

THE COLOURED CLOAKS OF PROTECTION

Let your child use their imagination and see themselves wrapping the cloak around them. This visualisation can help your child to feel safe, secure and allow them to maintain their space.

White Cloak
If your child chooses the White cloak then they like cleanliness and the feeling of purity around them. Your child needs to keep away from harsh energies, crowds and polluted atmospheres. They need guided visualisation's, essential oils and regular salt baths.

Pink Cloak
Pink dissolves negativity and anger. The pink cloak will be helpful when in negative situations. It helps the child to feel secure and loved.

Purple Cloak
A Purple cloak makes them feel safe and protected. This colour helps them to keep balanced and focused.

Green Cloak
The colour Green will be healing and calming for your child.

Golden Cloak
Helps your child to absorb new information and enhances communication. Assists in mental agility and enhances learning, wisdom and knowledge. They need regular guided visulisaitons, and using their imagination daily.

Indigo Cloak
Helps a sensitive child to feel safe and protected when around harsh energies. It helps your child with inner calmness, self-esteem, self-acceptance and self-trust.

Rainbow Cloak
By choosing this cloak your child has an ability to spread love and joy to others. These children are very giving, so remember to help them recharge themselves through, nature, quite time, love and guided visualizations

WATER FEATURES

Water represents our emotional feelings. Each picture holds a different emotion and shows you how your child is dealing and reacting to relationships at this moment. The calmer the water, the calmer the child.

Water fountain
Releasing of their emotions. Your child may benefit from a good cry and cuddle. Allow your child to release through creativity.

Waterfall
Releasing and outpouring of emotions. May also need cleansing of the mind and body through good food, exercise and nature.

Stream with rocks down the sides
Your child can be strong and single minded and they can keep their emotions to themselves. So give your child opportunities to express themselves. Will often open up better to someone other than a parent.

Bird bath
Your child likes to share their emotions. Listen when they ask for help.
Your child may also need to feel more freedom in their life at this present time.

Lake with mountain behind
Your child needs calming, balance and stability. They would benefit by having a more settled home life and also having a routine.

Lily pond
Your child is sensitive in regards to areas of love and feeling loved. They need one to one attention by a parent.

Swimming pool with diving board
Your child needs more fun and playtime in their daily lives. They also like to dive straight into their emotions and have no fear of sharing and expressing how they feel.

TREES

Trees represent strength, endurance, security, protection and shelter.

Apple Tree

Your child seeks truth, love, peace, beauty, honesty, creativity, happiness, and magical things. Your child needs to replenish their mind and body through a healthy diet. They would benefit from meditation as this will allow them to tap into their imagination and release any blockages that they have within themselves at this time. They would benefit from a more open communication about how they are truly feeling. A good Bach Flower Remedy would be Crab Apple.

Blossom Tree

Your child is changing and growing daily. They will need extra guidance and support from their parents while they are coming into full bloom and joy. Spend as much time with your child as you feel is necessary as time is a valuable gift.

Oak Tree

Your child is in a good strong place. They have a lot of inner strength and confidence. Help them maintain this through your support and encouragement

Shading Tree

Your child needs to feel protected and balanced. Help them feel safe and secure. Encourage your child to use their imagination and remind them of how to use the cloaks that are mentioned on page 4.

Little Tree

Your child needs a lot of encouragement, support and acceptance. Find ways to raise your child's self esteem.

Bare Tree

Your child needs a lot of love and nurturing. They will need a lot of individual attention, support and opportunities to socialize more.

Pine Tree

Your child is very strong and resilient; however they can occasionally show rigidity and inflexibility.
Your child needs patience and understanding. They would benefit from having a routine and predictablity.

Willow Tree

Your child may need time out and a calming environment. Your child also needs to tap into their imagination.
Try using Meditation, Yoga or Thai Chi

FLOWERS
Flowers are nature's gift. Using Essential oils and Bach Flower Remedies can help soothe, calm and balance your child's emotions.

Daffodil
Your child needs honesty and truth. They need people to be upfront with them at all times. They can sense it when people are not honest and open.

Rose
By choosing the rose your child needs deep love. They may also need time out to nurture themselves. They might be feeling unloved at this time.

Sunflower
Your child needs openness, warmth and cheerfulness. They just want to be happy and to be around others who are happy. They have a positive outlook on life.

Tulips
Your child is very caring and they like to give and receive lots of affection. Your child has a tendency to seek perfection and can become frustrated when perfection isn't achieved.

Buttercups
Your child maybe lacking in self worth and self-love. Communication is the main focus of your attention. They need space to express themselves e.g. through art, drama, play & singing etc..

Poppy
Your child likes a lot of freedom, independence and time out to use their imagination. They would benefit from the use of regular mindful techniques.

Daisy
Your child is happy and uplifting to be around and has a freshness about them. They are extremely loyal, patient and innocent.

Pansy
Your child enjoys being with others and they need kindness and love to feel secure. They are quite deep thinkers and need encouragement to open up.

Blue bell
Your child needs constant reassurance as they are susceptible to sad feelings at this time. They need to spend a lot of time in nature to feel uplifted, grounded and calm. You can also use positive affirmations, Mindfulness, Bach flower remedies and guided visualisations.

Jasmine
Your child needs more independence if they haven't already got it. Your child may also need to maintain their space. Spending a lot of their time with others might become too draining for them and it may effect their mood. Guided visualisations & Essential bath oils will help.

Snowdrops
Represents new beginnings and hope. Maybe your child is going through a change and needs to stay optimistic. Positive affirmations can help with this child.

CRYSTAL MEANINGS

Children love crystals. Bring crystals into their daily lives. They help them to feel safe, protected and special.

Amethyst
It's a stone that makes your child feel safe and protected. It is a strong healing stone.

Rose Quartz
It's a loving, calming and nurturing stone. Your child needs lots of love and support at this time. You can place the stone under your child's pillow for a good nights sleep.

Citrine
It's a powerful cleansing stone, enhances creative abilities and energises the body.

Clear Quartz
One of the most powerful healing stones. It harmonizes the body and clears the mind. Helps to overcome ones fears and gives confidence, protection and clarity.

Aquamarine
Calming; reduces stress and quietens the mind, gives courage, helps sensitive people, helps with blocked communication and with self expression.

Black Tourmaline
Eases stress; promotes relaxation and grounding, improves sleep, gives protection from outside influences and clears negative thoughts.

Sodalite
Wonderful for communication problems. Helps with intuition and clears electromagnetic pollution.

Pyrite
Helps to balance a child's energies and keeps them grounded. Great for children with ADD & ADHD.

Turquoise
A protective and healing stone. It helps with communication, stabilizes mood swings and brings about inner calmness. Particularly good for children with Autism and ADHD.

Jade
A calming and balancing stone: bringing serenity, positivity, love, protection, healing, emotional healing, compassion and peace. Helps remove negative thought patterns. Creates harmony, focus and self assurance.

ANIMAL FRIENDS

The animals represent different characteristics, qualities and behaviours that your child may be showing at this moment in time.

Butterfly
The Butterfly symbolizes transformation. Your child will be going through some positive changes, like coming into their own. If your child is quiet and reserved then you are about to see a shift taking place in them; they will be coming out of themselves with a new sense of growth.

Dolphin
The Dolphin symbolizes playfulness and harmony. Your child will have a great connection to water and sea life, be sensitive to people's feelings and their surroundings and be kind and caring to others. At the moment they just want to have fun!

Lion
The Lion symbolizes strength, courage, and self confidence. Your child may need courage at this time. They may be lacking in confidence and need reassurance that all is ok. Your child will enjoy playing in groups at this time and you will find that they normally take the lead when in the company of other children.

Elephant
The Elephant symbolizes patience, protectiveness and, family. By choosing the elephant your child has a strong intuitive side. He or she may be stubborn at times as they really want to see something through to the end. They may need more confidence at this time and will enjoy being surrounded by others, especially family.

Peacock
The Peacock symbolizes kindness, confidence, nurturing and awakening. They walk and hold themselves like royalty; they are intuitive, sensitive and are kind to others. Your child will either be confident or may need extra confidence at this time. They need a lot of nurturing.

Deer
The Deer symbolizes sensitivity and gentleness. Your child may feel over sensitive, nervous and vulnerable at this time. Therefore quiet time is needed for them to recharge. Going into nature will really help them to bring about balance and inner harmony. They will need to keep away from harsh energies and certain foods.

Birds
Birds symbolize freedom, releasing limitations, and creativity. Your child may feel controlled, not being allowed to expresses him or herself fully. Because birds represent creativity, they will need to take part in creative projects to allow them to fully express themselves. They will also be sensitive to the feelings of people around them.

Rabbit
The Rabbit symbolizes growth and family. Your child will be sensitive and artistic and will love to spend time with the family. They will benefit from nature and being outside and running freely in the parks. A healthy nutritious diet full of vegetables is important to them right now.

Hedgehog
The Hedgehog symbolizes resourcefulness, protection, gentleness and wisdom. Your child can be very calm, cool and practical at the moment. They can hold their space very well and stay focused on where they are going. Your child will connect very much to outdoor life and benefit from lots of time alone.

Owl
The Owl symbolizes wisdom, knowledge, transition and protection. Your child has a strong inner awareness when it comes to others. They have a deep understanding of life. They think a lot and like to learn as much as they can about life. They use their intuition daily.

Fox
The Fox symbolizes flexibility, cleverness, quick thinking, adaptability, and passion. Your child is very focused when they need to be and determined to finish what their heart truly desires. They are adaptable to circumstances and changes but can also be a child of habit in their home environment. They may want to blend into the background at the moment and just observe what's going on around them.

Squirrel
The Squirrel symbolises the need to play. Your child may need to socialize more with others or may need to be resourceful. May also need balance.

MAGICAL FRIENDS

Wizard
If your child has chosen the Wizard then they need to feel safe and protected. A Wizard will always keep negativity away and help them feel empowered and strong. Help you child to understand that they are safe and protected.

Fairy
The Fairy represents the elemental kingdom which looks over and protects Mother Nature. If your child chose the Fairy as their partner for the garden then your child will love the outdoors and animals and will have a full inner understanding of Mother Nature and how they can protect her. Fairy elementals like to have lots of fun and can, from time to time, become ungrounded. Allow your child to stomp around in the grass barefooted.

Unicorn
The Unicorn represents purity, strength, wisdom and grace. It has a close association to the elemental kingdom. If your child has chosen the unicorn for its garden then your child will be creative, imaginative, nature loving and intuitive. Allow your child to nurture these qualities.

Dragon
The Dragon represents protection, strength, courage and mystery. By choosing the Dragon your child may need protection and encouragement to overcome their fears.

Phoenix
The Phoenix symbolizes the mystical, rebirth, purification, honesty and loyalty. It represents the renewal of life. Your child has deep inner wisdom and knowledge. They pride themselves on loyalty and honesty and have high values. They may be going through a time of great change.

Mermaid
Mermaids represent strong intuition, emotions, beauty, privacy and independence. If your child chooses the mermaid then they will love to be near water, will have strong emotional feelings, will want to be free within themselves and what they are doing. They may wish to spend time alone.

Angel
Angel represents healing, love and protection. Your child will be very sensitive, intuitive, loving and caring and needs protection from harsh energies. Your child can carry a clear quartz crystal or take Bach Flower Rescue Remedy to help them.

Knight
Knights represent protection and courage; they are truth seekers and trust worthy. If your child has chosen the knight then they will be extremely protective of others especially family members. They will try to keep the peace but at the same time always wish for the truth to be shown. They may take a leading role at school or when around other children.

Buddha
The Buddha represents meditation, quiet time, relaxation, and breath. By choosing the Buddha your child will need time out; there is too much going on at present and they now need some quiet time to relax and to be more focused. They would benefit from regular meditation.

Alien
If your child has chosen the Alien to be in his or her garden then they are strong, quiet, sensitive, introverted and very kind and helpful to others.

FRIENDS & FAMILY
Your child may choose one of the friends or family members because they either have a special connection or feel safe and loved or they may have an issue with a person that needs to be resolved.

My Magical Garden Guided Visualisation

The benefits of guided visualisations for children include an overall sense of calmness, increased concentration, and improved flexibility. As a family-time activity, such as listening to a guided visualisation CD together or group visualisations with children, it can strengthen bonds, improve the quality of relationships and create a pathway to open communication.

This guided visualisation will take you on a journey to your magical mystical garden where you can connect with magical friends and creatures. Children will calm their mind and connect to the energy of their body. By using the power of guided imagery it will help your child to become calmer and happier within themselves.

Love & Light
Terri & Jacqui